ideals®
VALENTINE

Vol. 48, No. 1

Publisher, Patricia A. Pingry
Editor, Nancy J. Skarmeas
Editorial Assistant, LaNita Kirby
Art Director, Patrick McRae
Contributing Editor, Bonnie Aeschliman

ISBN 0-8249-1088-5

IDEALS—Vol. 48, No. 1 February MCMXCI IDEALS (ISSN 0019-137X) is published eight times a year: February, March, May, June, August, September, November, December by IDEALS PUBLISHING CORPORATION, P.O. Box 148000, Nashville, Tenn. 37214. Second-class postage paid at Nashville, Tennessee, and additional mailing offices. Copyright © MCMXCI by IDEALS PUBLISHING CORPORATION. POSTMASTER: Send address changes to Ideals, Post Office Box 148000, Nashville, Tenn. 37214-8000. All rights reserved. Title IDEALS registered U.S. Patent Office.

SINGLE ISSUE—$4.95
ONE-YEAR SUBSCRIPTION—eight consecutive issues as published—$19.95
TWO-YEAR SUBSCRIPTION—sixteen consecutive issues as published—$35.95
Outside U.S.A., add $6.00 per subscription year for postage and handling.

ACKNOWLEDGMENTS

TO HER by Edgar A. Guest: used by permission of the Estate; ONLY LOVE by Ann Thompson Jester from *WHERE VIOLETS GROW*, published by Banner Press, Inc., 1988. Used by permission. Our special thanks to the following authors whose addresses could not be found: To Marie De Winstanley Parks for BECAUSE OF YOU; To Anna M. Priestly for WINTER EVENING; To Marie Hunter Dawson for TO YOU; To Grace R. Ballard for WINGS IN THE SNOW; To Mabel Lindsey Vick for OLD LACE VALENTINE; To Esther F. Thom for THE SWEETEST VALENTINE; To Ada Downey Potter for SIGHTS AND SOUNDS OF WINTER; and To Clyde Edwin Tuck for ALL FOR YOU and SINCE I FOUND YOU.

Four-color separations by Rayson Films, Inc., Waukesha, Wisconsin

Printing by The Banta Company, Menasha, Wisconsin

The paper used in this publication meets the minimum requirements of American National Standard for Information Sciences—Permanence of Paper for Printed Library Materials, ANSI Z39.48-1984.

Unsolicited manuscripts will not be returned without a self-addressed stamped envelope.

Valentine's Day

Margaret Rorke

Caught in a climate
    so callous and cold,
Born of a bearing
    benumbing and bold,
There is a pause
    that defies winter's way,
Known unto people
    as Valentine's Day.

Not in the summer
    when weather is warm,
Nor in the season
    that's senseless to storm,
Not when the birds and
    the blooms are their best—
No, it arrives when the
    days are distressed.

This is symbolic—
    a heart where it shows,
Melting for others
    their mantle of snows,
Giving life's ribs
    an affectionate shove.
Such is the soul
    and the substance of love.

Photo Opposite
VALENTINE BOUQUET
Fotoconcept Inc.

Valentine

Carol Bessent Hayman

February brought
The world a valentine:
Trees edged in icy lace,
A blue velvet sky;
Winter-bright veil of ruffles
Around the slender throat of day.

And when dusk came,
The sable-coated arms of night
Reached out and placed
One perfect star
In heaven's hair.

Photo Opposite
WINTER TREES
FPG International

Painting Overleaf
SLEIGH RIDE
by Adrian Kupan
Superstock

Valentine Glow

There is a day in February
   when hearts are so aglow
That little thoughts of springtime
   reach out to melt the snow.

'Tis love for one another that
   through cold and gray can shine;
'Tis love for one another that
   makes a valentine.

Carole Ann Johnston
Sergeant Bluff, Iowa

This Valentine

This valentine with trim of ribboned lace
Is under glass and in a golden frame,
Showing a dimpled cupid's laughing face
As with a crimson arrow he takes his aim.
His target is a heart as red as flame,
Above whose curving form, a soft white dove
Flies with a note that bears an inscribed name
And climbing roses twine to bloom above
A golden verse sent by my own true love.

E'Lane Carlisle Murray
Corpus Christi, Texas

8

Reflections

To My Valentine

Snowflakes form designs
Of lace to edge your valentine.
Blue is added from the skies—
A color touch to match your eyes.
The sun of afternoon is cold,
Yet tints with warmth in glints of gold.

Red that leaps in a glowing flame
Of joy, at mention of your name,
The beat of winter wings, of dove
And other birds to sing my love
Will complete this work of art,
With this exception, dear—my heart!

E. Cole Ingle
Mansfield, Ohio

Editor's Note: Readers are invited to submit unpublished, original poetry, short anecdotes, and humorous reflections on life for possible publication in future *Ideals* issues. Please send copies only; manuscripts will not be returned. Writers receive $10 for each published submission. Send material to: "Readers' Reflections," Ideals Publishing Corporation, P.O. Box 140300, Nashville, TN 37214-0300.

Valentines

Some valentines may rightly be
What you are best at giving.
You know what is your specialty,
What adds to joy in living.

It may be just a sincere smile
When someone is despairing.
It's then that someone sees in you
Reflection of God's caring.

Virginia R. Hendrick
Flint, Michigan

ALCHEMY

Maureen Cannon

Black branches stitched
With white, and white
On white the birches,
Icy bright,
Bewitched and silent . . .

Suddenly
A sound of winter's
Children, free
At last and racing
Homeward. High,
Alive, their laughter
Tears the sky
Wide open, wrenches
From its spell
The sleeping street . . .
And carousels
Of tiny figures,
Spinning, shake
A secret silent
World awake!

Sights and Sounds of Winter

Ada D. Potter

Sharpening its icicles, winter sketches
    bare branches against a cobalt sky.
And the savage North Wind striding down
    the valley, sculpts fantastic shapes,
Then turns and gently pulls a blanket
    over sleeping flowers.

Across the silent whiteness, a hieroglyphic
    pattern spells out the names of countless
       fur-clad creatures.
Pursued by a brilliant, icy moon and one huge star,
    the sun hurries down the sky and vanishes
       in blazing splendor.

Then from a piney thicket, an owl hoots,
    and a fox barks at a frightened hare.
My feet squeak on a snow path—
    each breath is etched upon the frosty air,
Until the scent of wood smoke lures me in
    to dream of spring, and flower seeds,
       beside the dying fire.

WINTER SCENE
H. Armstrong Roberts

Ina Mackey, Photographer

Because of You

Marie deWinstanley Parks

Because of you
The floor of my heart
Is paved with sunbeams,
Warming every minute
Of every golden day.

The thermal robe
Of security
Clothes me and the flowers
Of my memory
Never fade away.

Soft music fills
The velvet night
And peace enfolds my soul
Because of you!

Love Is a Rose

Nell Thompson Miller

Love is a rose
Beginning to bloom,
Slowly opening,
Filling a room
With beauty and calm
Wherever it blows,
Love is a rose.

Love is a rose
Of many hues:
Soft to the touch,
As the heart renews
Each tender promise,
One suddenly knows
Love is a rose.

Ina Mackey, Photographer

15

Overleaf
OLD-FASHIONED VALENTINE
Superstock

To my Valentine

TRAVELER'S *Diary*

Marian H. Tidwell

The *Mississippi Queen* and her sister ship, the *Delta Queen*.

The Queen of the Mississippi

Someday, they'll build the biggest steamboat the world has ever known, and she'll be long, white, and gleaming in the sunshine with her twin black stacks. And that one shall be the Queen of the Mississippi.

Mark Twain

At the height of the American steamboat era, Mark Twain imagined a boat that would outdo them all—a single steamboat that would encompass all the charm, beauty, and grandeur of the time and the place that had so captured his own creative imagination. Today, though the era of the steamboat has passed, the ship that Twain envisioned does ply the waters of the Mississippi.

Built in 1976, the aptly-named *Mississippi Queen* turns its giant paddlewheel through the rivers of the American heartland, transporting travelers back in time to the days of Mark Twain and the romantic reign of the great American steamboats. The *Mississippi Queen* is no disappointment to the modern, idealized image of steamboat travel. The paddlewheel gently propels the ship at approximately eight miles per hour. This slow pace reminds the traveler that on this trip it is the journey, and not the destination, that matters.

And that journey can be many things. On board there is both time and space for individual pursuits, such as an afternoon spent watching the

18

unfolding scene on the river bank, an evening listening to Dixieland jazz, or a romantic night strolling on the moonlit deck. And when the moods strikes, there is always opportunity for travelers to get together. One day might feature a celebration of the showboat, with songs and performances from the days of these great traveling troupes. Another could be devoted to a visit from the steamboat's own "Mark Twain," an impersonator who makes the rounds entertaining passengers with stories from the life and fiction of one of our greatest authors. And at least one day should include a session with the resident "riverlorian," whose sole purpose on board is to share facts and legends about life and work on the more than 11,000 steamboats that once traveled America's rivers.

The *Mississippi Queen* operates year round, with tours on both the upper and lower Mississippi as well as sections of the Ohio, Cumberland, and Tennessee rivers. Although trips originate at points all along these rivers, New Orleans is a particularly appropriate starting point, especially when winter chills the northern climates. A night in this historic, romantic city sets the mood for a wonderful tour through the southern Mississippi, with stops at Baton Rouge and St. Francisville, Louisiana, and Vicksburg and Natchez, Mississippi.

The accommodations aboard the *Mississippi Queen* are similar to that of a grand hotel. But do not be misled by the ship's list of modern conveniences. This is not a hotel, nor is it simply a cruise ship. Even with all the comforts of modern life, the feel of the ship remains true to

Employees in period costume greet the steamboat.

the nineteenth century and the pace of life on the river. On a quiet afternoon, when the only sound is the lapping of water through the paddlewheel, it is not difficult to imagine Huck Finn boarding his raft beneath the cypress and sycamores that line the water's edge, preparing for a journey down river.

And that is what a trip aboard the *Mississippi Queen* is all about—experiencing the charm and romance of another time. It is often said that a cruise aboard this beautiful steamboat is much like a visit to the fine home of an old friend. The atmosphere is warm and friendly, and the mood is one of relaxed camaraderie. Every effort is made to welcome guests into the era of the great American steamboats. The result is a leisurely escape from the worries of everyday life and an unforgettable travel experience.

The *Mississippi Queen* on the open river.

Photos courtesy of the Delta Queen Steamboat Company.

Shall I Compare Thee?

William Shakespeare

Shall I compare thee to a summer's day?
Thou art more lovely and more temperate:
Rough winds do shake the darling buds of May,
And summer's lease hath all too short a date:
Sometime too hot the eye of heaven shines,
And often is his gold complexion dimm'd;
And every fair from fair sometime declines,
By chance, or nature's changing course untrimmed;
But thy eternal summer shall not fade,
Nor lose possession of that fair thou ow'st,
Nor shall death brag thou wander'st in his shade,
When in eternal lines to time thou grow'st;
   So long as men can breathe, or eyes can see,
   So long lives this, and this gives life to thee.

Jerome Kern and *Showboat*

In 1926, *Showboat,* a novel by American author Edna Ferber, held a steady spot on the best seller list. The novel was a fictionalized account of life on a Mississippi riverboat, complete with romance, adventure, political intrigue, and high-stakes gambling.

Among the countless readers impressed by Ferber's vivid tale was the composer Jerome Kern. Within the world of Ferber's novel Kern envisioned the makings of a musical, and he announced his plans to write the score and bring *Showboat* to the stage.

Today, Kern's decision appears both brilliant and unquestionable. *Showboat* has become an American classic. Its songs and characters are part of our popular culture. But in 1926, Kern's plans to put Ferber's story to music met with objections from all quarters. This was simply not acceptable subject matter for musical comedy.

Jerome Kern was already considered somewhat of a musical pioneer. He had challenged the typical American dependence upon European musical forms and traditions and had turned, instead, to the common elements of American life for inspiration. Thus, instead of the typical production of the twenties, made up of extravagant costumes and exaggerated characters with little or no unifying plot and theme, Kern had written musicals that revolved around real people in recognizable situations, with the music complementing the flow of the plot.

His choice of *Showboat*, however, appeared to many of his friends and associates to be taking his taste for "realism" one step too far. Not only was this common American life, it was the coarse life of gamblers and minstrels and poor southern blacks. These were elements of the American experience outside the mainstream. Were these unsavory characters to be the stuff of a major musical production?

Certainly, Kern answered, and he went to work. Enlisting the help of Oscar Hammerstein II with the lyrics and P. G. Wodehouse with the script, Kern prepared his version of *Showboat* for the stage. And if audiences held out any last hope that this would be a "sanitized" version of the Ferber novel, they were to be disappointed. Merging his classical training with the sounds and moods of the Blues and Negro spirituals, Kern brought Edna Ferber's colorful, three-dimensional characters to life. He revealed the flaws and scars of the riverboat people, certainly. But with powerful, unforgettable songs like "Ol' Man River," "My Bill," and "Can't Help Lovin' Dat Man," he also revealed their humanity and dignity.

Objections to Kern's plan, needless to say, soon faded. *Showboat* ran for 572 consecutive performances and was revived several times. Kern's musical was also twice made into a motion picture. Today, few Americans exist who have not seen the musical or the movie or heard the songs performed.

In 1941, at the request of conductor Arthur Rodzinski, Kern composed a symphonic version of *Showboat*, to be performed by the New York Philharmonic Orchestra at Carnegie Hall. After fifteen years, things had come full circle. The characters of the Mississippi riverboat who were once considered too coarse, too "real," for the musical stage were now celebrated in grand style in the most proper and correct of musical settings. Through his music, Kern had revealed the majesty and dignity in the ordinary lives of the people who lived, worked, and traveled on the river. In so doing he had bestowed upon the musical a new, distinctively American form.

Nancy Skarmeas

To My Loving Husband

Anne Bradstreet

If ever two were one, then surely we;
If ever man were loved by wife, then thee;
If ever wife were happy in a man,
Compare with me, ye women if you can.
I prize your love more than whole mines of gold,
Or all the riches that the earth doth hold.
My love is such that rivers cannot quench,
Nor ought but love from thee give recompense.
Your love is such I can no way repay;
The heavens reward thee manifold, I pray:
Then while we love, in love let's so persevere
That when we live no more we may love ever.

Photo Opposite
ROSES AND LACE
Larry Lefever from
Grant Heilman Photography, Inc.

ALL FOR YOU

Clyde Edwin Tuck

I shall not greatly care if nevermore
The ships return that I sent out to sea,
Or fortune frowns and bars her iron door,
If your sustaining love remains with me.

It is your love that saves me from despair,
That gives me courage to keep up the fight;
With you I boldly face fate's larger dare,
And your unswerving faith shall guide me right.

I could not falter, looking in your eyes,
Through which your soul shines steadfastly and true;
Success and fame and deeds of high emprise
I undertake, not for myself, but you.

SINCE I FOUND YOU

Clyde Edwin Tuck

I was impatient till each day was done
    that failed to bring my heart's ideal to view;
Clouds gathered and obscured life's morning sun,
    but since we met, the gray has changed to blue.

Since I found you my days are never drear—
    across my bright world blows the breath of May;
The birds send wavering shafts of song to cheer
    my soul, which joins their lilting roundelay.

Once more in Nature's arteries there flows
    spring's ichor that brings life to plains and hills,
And on the hearthstone of my heart now glows
    the fire of love, and peace my bosom fills.

SOMEONE THERE

Georgia B. Adams

Someone waiting on the threshold
    as I walk my homeward way
Is the most I ask in return
    for the labors of my day.

Someone there to bid me welcome,
    one to smile, to lift, to share;
Just someone to really live for;
    someone there to love and care.

'Twixt the four walls of my homestead
    just a cheery word or two
From a loved one is uplifting,
    helps to bring back skies of blue.

So the most I ask in return
    for the labors of the day
Is someone standing on the threshold
    as I walk my homeward way.

Photo Opposite
FLOWERS IN KITCHEN
Fotoconcept, Inc.

A SLICE OF LIFE

Edgar A. Guest

To Her

"To the mother of my children
    And the faithful wife o' mine,"
That's the line that I shall scribble
    On a simple valentine,
Just to sort o' reassure her
    In an old man's blundering way,
That I'm always thinking of her
    Through the troubles of the day.

"To the mother of my children,
    And the faithful wife o' mine,"
That's the way that I shall greet her
    With some simple valentine,
And her eyes will start to gleamin'
    And her heart go pit-a-pat,
For there isn't any title
    That would please her more than that.

So it's just that way I'll greet her,
    Just to sort o' let her know
That she's still the same old sweetheart
    That she was long years ago;
That there's no one any fairer
    Than my early valentine,
Now the mother of my children
    And the faithful wife o' mine.

Edgar A. Guest began his career in 1895 at the age of fourteen. His column was syndicated in over 300 newspapers and he became known as "The Poet of the People."

Special Valentine

Kay Hoffman

I have a little valentine
  so precious and so dear
No other valentine on earth
  could bring my heart more cheer.

I watch her from my windowpane,
  her little face so bright,
In marshmallow mounds of drifted snow,
  she finds a sheer delight.

I bow my head in prayer;
  I give thanks to God above,
And I ask him to watch over
  this little one I love.

Of all my cherished valentines,
  the dearest one I know
Is my little girl in her snowsuit
  tumbling in the snow!

CHILD IN SNOW
Superstock

The Sweetest Valentine

Esther F. Thom

Two paper hearts were cut just so,
And tied together with a bow.

These little hearts were colored red,
And one had printed words that said,
"Dear Grandma and dear Grandpa, too,
I love you very much, I do."

It hangs upon the kitchen wall—
Our sweetest valentine of all.

Mother's Valentine

Virginia Blanck Moore

The words don't go where they belong—
They wander here and there.
The pasting's also less than neat—
But does a mother care?

Indeed she cares not one small whit,
For the words say, "I love you",
And the hug and kiss her child bestows
With the message say it's true.

She would not trade a valentine
Designed with artist's taste
For this loving little masterpiece
Of sprawling words and paste.

Valentine Treats

Chocolate is one of life's great pleasures, and there is no better time to give in to its allure than on Valentine's Day. Pictured at right are four ways to say "I love you" with chocolate: a decorated chocolate cake, mousse-filled chocolate cupcakes, and the two special recipes featured below, Peppermint Patty Cookies and Peanut Butter and Chocolate Hearts.

Peanut Butter and Chocolate Hearts

1 cup semi-sweet or milk chocolate chips
2 tablespoons shortening, divided (do not substitute butter, margarine, or oil)
1 cup peanut butter chips
   Heart-shaped ice cube trays or mold

In small microwave-proof bowl combine chocolate chips with 1 tablespoon shortening. Microwave at high (100%) for 1 minute; stir. Microwave at high for 30 seconds or until melted and smooth when stirred. Spoon into heart-shaped ice cube tray or mold, filling each 1/2-full. Tap molds to remove air bubbles and smooth surface. Chill 10 to 15 minutes to partially set chocolate.

Meanwhile, in a small microwave-proof bowl, combine peanut butter chips with 1 tablespoon shortening. Microwave at high for 1 minute; stir. Microwave at high for 30 seconds or until melted and smooth when stirred. Spoon onto chocolate layer; tap to smooth surface. Chill several hours or until firm. Invert tray or mold and tap lightly to release candies. Makes about 10 candies.

Peppermint Patty Cookies

2/3 cup butter or margarine, softened
1 cup sugar
1 egg
1/2 teaspoon vanilla extract
1 1/2 cups all-purpose flour
1/3 cup unsweetened cocoa
1/2 teaspoon baking soda
1/4 teaspoon salt
3 tablespoons milk

Bite-size chocolate covered
   peppermint patties
Decorator Frosting (recipe follows)

In large mixer bowl cream butter and sugar; add egg and vanilla, blending well. Combine flour, cocoa, baking soda, and salt; add to creamed mixture alternately with milk, blending well. Chill dough about 1 hour or until firm enough to handle. (Dough will be a little soft.) Heat oven to 350°. Shape small portions of dough around peppermint patties, completely covering the candy. Place on lightly greased cookie sheet; flatten slightly and crimp with tines of fork around edge, if desired. Bake 10 to 12 minutes or until set. Cool 1 minute on cookie sheet; remove to wire rack. Cool completely. Write valentine messages on cookies with decorator frosting.

Decorator Frosting

3 tablespoons butter or margarine
2 cups confectioners' sugar
1/8 teaspoon salt
2-3 tablespoons milk
1/2 teaspoon vanilla extract
   Food coloring

In small mixer bowl cream butter or margarine, confectioners' sugar, and salt alternately with milk and vanilla. Beat until smooth and creamy; tint a pastel color.

Bonnie Aeschliman is a teacher of occupational home economics and a freelance food consultant. She lives in Wichita, Kansas, with her husband and their two children.

Photo Opposite
Clockwise from left to right: Chocolate Pecan Torte, Peanut Butter and Chocolate Hearts, Peppermint Patty Cookies, and Chocolate Dream Cups. Courtesy of the Hershey Foods Corporation.

Recipes developed by the Hershey Kitchens and provided courtesy of Hershey Foods Corporation.

MY MOTHER, MY VALENTINE

Barbara Smalley

When I was pregnant with my second child, other parents of two or more youngsters warned me that I'd never do as much to herald my second child's arrival as I did for my first. I turned a deaf ear to their remarks, until I realized that my number two son was nearly six weeks old, and I had yet to purchase a baby book for him. Feeling guilty, I rushed to the store and chose one with a big teddy bear on the cover. It wasn't until I had printed my son's name and birth date on the first page that I realized I had purchased a baby book for adoptive parents.

Laughing at my mistake, I called my mother. "Can you believe that?" I asked. "And it was expensive, too. Should I buy another one?" Mom laughed and answered, "Maybe you should. Otherwise, you may have a hard time later convincing him that he wasn't adopted. You know when kids grow up thinking or knowing that they are adopted, they can sometimes develop a complex."

Didn't I know it! I was adopted at birth by the woman on the other end of that telephone line. She and my dad had never hidden that fact from me; indeed, hearing how I was "chosen" was always one of my favorite stories as a child. My adoptive parents wanted me desperately, and they showered me with so much love that I don't recall ever regretting being adopted.

Neither can I recall ever wondering about my biological parents until I grew up and faced motherhood myself. Thrilled as I was about having a child, I was terrified of giving birth, and when my doctor asked for a complete family medical history, I fell apart. Were there any rare diseases in my family tree? What did my parents look like, and whom would my child resemble? Finally, I became convinced that the parents who had given me up twenty-nine years earlier would want to know they were about to become grandparents.

Obsessed with finding my biological parents, I sent my name to a half-dozen organizations that match children with parents, and then I sat by the phone and loitered by the mailbox waiting for answers to my growing list of questions.

Meanwhile, my adoptive mother was ecstatic about my pregnancy. When I confounded her with questions, she always found an answer. She lectured me on what to eat, and sent me clippings of articles about birth and babies. Her overwhelming concern and care soon led me to feel as if I were giving her the pregnancy she had never had.

Months flew by, and when the baby was born, my biological parents remained a mystery. I delivered a strapping baby boy—normal, healthy, and the image of his father. Mom flew for a visit the day I got home from the hospital and spent a week giving me and my husband a crash course on infant care.

After my mother left, and after my husband returned to work, I began to grasp for the first time the true meaning of motherhood. Granted, an infant must be carried in the

womb and pushed into the world by someone, but it is the one who paces and rocks and nurtures and loves who deserves the coveted title of "mother."

I never found my biological parents. In fact, bonding with my new son soon dissolved my desire to search. When my mother adopted me, she had no idea from whom or where I came. Then and now she has loved me unconditionally. And I have this year's Valentine's Day card to remind me of that. The commercially-produced verse inside reads:

If we could have chosen
Any daughter in the world
For our own—
One with warmth and kindness
Intelligence and wit,
One we would have loved
From the moment we saw her—
We would have chosen you

"And we did," my mother had added at the bottom of the card. That says it all.

Child's Play

THE CHILDREN'S HOUR

Henry Wadsworth Longfellow

Between the dark and the daylight,
  when the night is beginning to lower,
Comes a pause in the day's occupations
  that is known as the Children's Hour.

I hear in the chamber above me
  the patter of little feet,
The sound of a door that is opened,
  and voices soft and sweet.

From my study I see in the lamplight,
  descending the broad hall stair,
Grave Alice and laughing Allegra,
  and Edith with golden hair.

A whisper, and then a silence:
  yet I know by their merry eyes
They are plotting and planning together
  to take me by surprise.

A sudden rush from the stairway,
  a sudden raid from the hall!
By three doors left unguarded
  they enter my castle wall!

They climb up into my turret
  o'er the arms and back of my chair;
If I try to escape, they surround me;
  they seem to be everywhere.

They almost devour me with kisses,
  their arms about me entwine,
Till I think of the Bishop of Bingen
  in his Mouse-Tower in the Rhine!

Do you think, O blue-eyed banditti,
  because you have scaled the wall,
Such an old mustache as I am
  is not a match for you all?

I have you fast in my fortress,
  and I will not let you depart,
But put you down into the dungeon
  in the round-tower of my heart.

And there I will keep you forever,
  Yes, forever and a day,
Till the wall shall crumble to ruin,
  And molder in dust away!

THROUGH MY WINDOW

Pamela Kennedy

The alarm goes off and I nudge my sleeping husband, who automatically hits the snooze bar on the clock radio. I snuggle close to him, revelling in these stolen moments before the day begins. I'm just dozing off when there's a knock on the bedroom door.

"Mom, did I tell you I was supposed to take heart cookies to school today for the Valentine's Day party?"

"What!?" I'm awake now, sitting up in bed, glaring at my ten-year-old. He stands defenseless at the door, grinning hopefully. "Do I look like a magician who can whip up three dozen heart cookies at the crack of dawn?" I am tempted to run through my "you-have-to-plan-ahead" speech, but I am discouraged by its lack of success in the past. "Go away," I mutter, climbing out of bed.

In the shower, I think of creative ways to make cookies out of what I have in my cupboard: macaroni and cheese, pudding, seasoned bread crumbs. I dry off and get dressed without a plan.

In the kitchen, I make bologna sandwiches and consider cutting the meaty circles into heart shapes and sending them to school, but I have only eight slices left. My seven-year-old joins me in the kitchen.

"Have you seen my valentines? I signed them all last night and they aren't anywhere! Do you think a burglar took them?"

I express my doubts about a valentine burglar and go to her room. The valentines are in a neat stack on her desk—under her nightgown.

"Boy, Mom, they weren't there a few minutes ago!" I express my doubts about that and head back to the kitchen.

Twenty minutes have passed and I am still without heart cookies. After dishing out two bowls of oatmeal, I decide to meditate over the contents of the cupboard. Perhaps a flash of inspiration will strike. Jello, soup, coffee, crackers, frosting, spaghetti sauce—Wait! I grab a box of graham crackers and the can of frosting. Under the cake pans I find an unused pastry tube I received last Christmas. In a bowl I tint the vanilla frosting bright pink. After filling the tube, I inscribe wiggly hearts on the graham cracker squares—three dozen of them. Then I place them carefully in a large flat box. There! I have passed another test. I have made the school party snack in fifteen morning-minutes!

My son inspects my work. "Um," he says tentatively, "I was hoping for something else. Mrs. Barnes made strawberry tarts last year."

Silently I hate Mrs. Barnes, and I suggest aloud that her son probably mentioned the party a few days before it happened. He gets the point and says no more.

The school bus honks. My son and daughter dash out the door. I am not thanked. I am not kissed good-bye. I run after my daughter with her bag full of valentines and hand them through the bus window. I wave as the bus pulls away and nobody waves back. They are busy giving valentines to friends.

Back inside I find a note propped next to my coffee cup. "Come back to bed," it says. I'm wide awake, I have packed two lunches, and I have made three dozen graham cracker cookies: why would I want to go back to bed now? But I smile because I know the author of the note, and I open the bedroom door.

There he sits, propped up on pillows against the headboard. There is a tray on the nightstand with two steaming mugs of coffee and a frilly heart-shaped box of expensive chocolates.

"What's this?" I inquire, warily.

He pats the pillow propped beside him and I sit down.

"This," he says, grinning, "is 'chocolates for breakfast'."

"Fattening," I reply, popping one in my mouth.

"Absolutely," he agrees, dipping one into his hot coffee.

"The kitchen is a mess," I add.

"I know," he says. "Will you be my valentine?"

"Mrs. Barnes sent in strawberry tarts last year and I sent in graham crackers with store-bought frosting."

He looks at me with twenty-two years of love in his eyes. "I'll bet Mrs. Barnes isn't having chocolates for breakfast!"

I giggle. "You are a crazy and wonderful person and yes, I will always be your valentine. Please pass the chocolates."

Pamela Kennedy is a freelance writer of short stories, articles, essays, and children's books. Married to a naval officer and mother of three children, she has made her home on both U.S. coasts and currently resides in Hawaii. She draws her material from her own experiences and memories, adding bits of imagination to create a story or mood.

To You

Marie Hunter Dawson

You make me think of lovely things,
The sky of depthless blue and boundless space,
Rose petals, crushed, emitting sweet perfume,
The velvet softness of a baby's face.

You make me think of dawn and singing birds,
Of streams that murmur gently on the air,
Of rare old books or strains of lovely song,
Of dew or moonbeams or a lock of hair.

You make me see the grandeur of a star,
The vast importance of an hour, a breath;
The power beneath a word, a glance, a step,
The sure impossibility of death.

You make me feel the faith of man,
The human heart's unfathomable love,
The value of a little hope and trust,
The nearness of the earth to the above.

When you are near, the sordid disappears,
And I aspire to live the life I should,
For in the tender sweetness of yourself
Is all that lifts me up and makes me good.

Angel Wings

Grace R. Ballard

When I was very young and snow
Lay soft and moist upon the frozen ground,
We played a game, as children have
Since time began, I know, wherein we found
Delight. Dressed warmly, our imaginings
Perceived within unbroken snow
Our childhood's simple dreams
Of angel wings.

Lying face upward on the smoothest place,
We raised our arms above our heads; and then
In graceful, undulating lines we swept
   them down
To sturdy, wool-clad sides again.
Upon arising, youth's strong patternings
Impressioned there, found in the depths
Of wind-swept snow where we had lain
The form of angel wings.

Long years have passed; and now
When frosted night-wind sings
Over the drifted fields, I think I hear
From far away a child's gay laughter
In the snow; and then, quite clear
The gentle stir of angel wings.

CRAFTWORKS

VALENTINE HEART DOOR HANGING

Materials Needed:

3 sheets tracing paper (11 x 17)
1 yard 2¼-inch red satin ribbon
3 yards ⅜-inch red satin ribbon
1 1-pound bag polyester stuffing
1 2-inch plastic ring
½ yard heart print fabric for large heart
¼ yard heart print fabric for medium heart
¼ yard heart print fabric for small heart
  Matching thread

Making Pattern Pieces:

Fold the tracing paper sheets in half and trace the half-heart patterns from this page, aligning the fold of the paper with the straight edge of the pattern. Be sure to trace the arrows onto each pattern piece.

With paper still folded, cut around heart. Repeat for three sizes. Unfold pattern pieces. You now have three different sized heart-shaped pattern pieces.

Cutting Pattern:

Fold fabric along grain. Pin tracing paper pattern pieces to fabric, making sure to align the arrows on pattern pieces with the grain of the fabric. Cut around patterns through both layers of fabric. You should now have two matching fabric hearts for each size.

Making Pillows:

With right sides of corresponding fabric hearts facing, stitch around edges with a half-inch seam allowance. Leave approximately 2 inches open on one side for stuffing. Clip seam and turn right side out. Stuff with polyester stuffing and slip stitch opening. Repeat for next two pillows.

Assembling Door Hanging:

Sew the 2¼-inch ribbon to the center of the back of the largest heart, leaving 1¼ inches of ribbon above stitching for attaching plastic ring. Sew the medium heart 3¼ inches below the bottom point of the large heart; repeat for the smallest heart, again allowing 3¼ inches below the bottom of the preceding heart.

Attach the plastic ring to the top length of ribbon by threading the ribbon through the ring from the front and sewing together behind to form a loop.

Finishing:

Make a loose bow with the ¼-inch ribbon and attach it to the top center of the largest heart. Leave the ends of the bow hanging as streamers across the front of the pillow. Cut an inverted "v" shape into the bottom of the larger ribbon to create a finished look.

Joan Alberstadt is a former commercial artist who now devotes her time to a home sewing and craft business. She lives with her husband and children in Nashville, Tennessee.

Country
CHRONICLE

———Margaret A. Jenkins———

I remember long ago,
Following Dad's footprints
Through the snow,
As he made a path
Down the street.
Along the way he would greet
His neighbors, who
Were shovelling too.

Laughingly I would
Slip and slide,
Trying to match
His longer stride.
Then we would rest
Amidst the swirling

Flakes of snow
And my tongue
Would catch the flakes
So cold and wet—
I can smell the
Fresh crisp air yet.

Fascinated I would watch
Cold smoke rings
Disappear at a touch.
My heart still sings
At the memory of
The crunching snow,
Those days with my father,
Long ago.

VALENTINE REMEMBRANCE

Louise Pugh Corder

Remember dear, when long ago
We walked through fields of fresh-fallen snow.
With hearts in tune and arms entwined,
You pledged your love, and I pledged mine.

Amid a wondrous world of white,
We spun fine dreams that winter night
And planned the life that we would share—
A perfect life, untouched by care.

You drew a huge heart in the snow,
Wrote love inside—our names below.
You held me in a warm embrace
As feathery flakes fell on my face.

Now gray heads close, we watch snow fall
On frosted lawn as we recall
When all our blissful dreams were young;
Our lives unspent, love's songs unsung.

We smile at how youth seldom knows
That there are thorns on every rose;
Maturity's often bought with tears,
Yet love grows richer through the years.

Photo Opposite
VALENTINE KEEPSAKES
H. Armstrong Roberts

COLLECTOR'S CORNER

Hummels

#47, The Goose Girl

#315, The Mountaineer

Hummels are ceramic figurines, usually images of innocent, wide-eyed children busily involved in everyday activities or simply enjoying the delights of nature. The delicate beauty of these figurines and the fascinating history of their creation make the Hummel an appealing and much sought-after collectible.

Berta Hummel was born on May 21, 1909, in the small, picturesque Bavarian town of Massing. She was known as a friendly, energetic, and inquisitive girl. Early in her life she demonstrated a love of drawing and sketching; and since the arts were an important part of her family's life, her talents were encouraged.

When she was eighteen years old, Berta enrolled in the Academy of Fine Arts in Munich. After graduating from the Academy, Berta joined a convent and began teaching school.

Surrounded each day by the children she loved, Berta—now known as Sister Maria Innocentia—found constant inspiration for her art. She related well to children and spent hours drawing pictures for them. It was not long before Berta became known for her artwork. Just one year after beginning to teach, Berta illustrated a collection of poems for children called *The Hummel Book*. And later that year she released her second book, *Sketch Me—Berta Hummel*.

These books allowed Berta to combine her two greatest loves—children and art. They also brought her recognition outside the convent

#264, 1971 Annual Plate

#265, 1972 Annual Plate

#266, 1973 Annual Plate

school. In 1934, Franz Goebel, of the W. Goebel Company, came across one of Berta's books. In her beautiful drawings of children, Goebel saw ideal subjects for ceramic figurines. Berta was skeptical at first. Her religious vows included a vow of poverty, and she was unwilling to sell her work for her own gain. After much consideration, she and Goebel worked out an arrangement for the convent to be paid for her work. In March of 1935 the first Hummel figurines were placed on the market, and they immediately became a popular collectible.

Hummel figurines are noted for their realistic detail and their subtle color and texture. Authentic Hummels bear both the signature of M.I. Hummel and the Goebel trademark. Six trademarks have been used since 1935. The earlier marks are favored, making the older editions the most highly prized. Berta Hummel's nickname was "Das Hummele," which means "busy bee". For this reason, a bee was used as part of the trademark from 1950 until 1979.

There are 450 designs of Hummels, and most are still in production today. Since large numbers of most figurines have been produced, there are still a great number in existence. Because of this, even the slightest damage significantly reduces the figurine's value as a collectible.

In 1971, the first Hummel Annual Plate was issued. These plates carry a representation of one of the figurine motifs. All annual plates have the year on the front and a border of five-point stars. Hummel plaques, bells, candy dishes, clocks, candle holders, lamp bases, and bookends are also produced, but the figurines continue to be of greatest interest and value as collectibles.

Though there are many of the figurines in existence today, they should only grow in value as the years pass. The endearing subjects and superior craftsmanship evident in all Hummels reflect the commitment of their creators, and guarantee their lasting value.

#127, The Doctor

#128, The Baker

#305, The Builder

#112, Just Reading

Carol Shaw Johnston, a public school teacher, writes articles and short stories. She lives with her family in Brentwood, Tennessee.

Old-Fashioned Valentine

Elisabeth Weaver Winstead

Today I mailed your valentine,
The delicate, sweet, old-fashioned kind,
All roses and forget-me-nots,
With tiny hearts entwined.

All filligree and filmy lace,
And limpid lines that sing
Of love that stays forever young
And faith unfaltering.

This token offering I make
Because my thoughts of you
Are tranquil, tender, treasured things—
Like violets in ribbons of blue,

Silver wings that shimmer,
And gold stars that glisten and shine.
And so to you, dear heart of mine,
I send this loving valentine.

Opposite
VALENTINE GREETINGS
Superstock

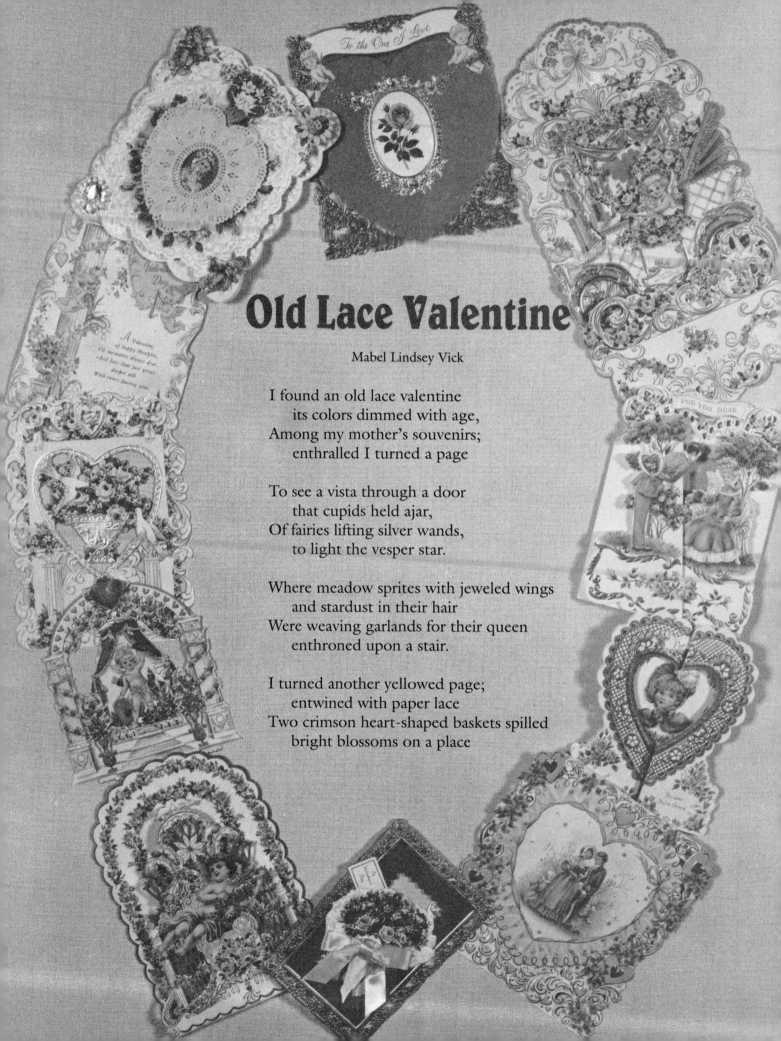

Old Lace Valentine

Mabel Lindsey Vick

I found an old lace valentine
    its colors dimmed with age,
Among my mother's souvenirs;
    enthralled I turned a page

To see a vista through a door
    that cupids held ajar,
Of fairies lifting silver wands,
    to light the vesper star.

Where meadow sprites with jeweled wings
    and stardust in their hair
Were weaving garlands for their queen
    enthroned upon a stair.

I turned another yellowed page;
    entwined with paper lace
Two crimson heart-shaped baskets spilled
    bright blossoms on a place

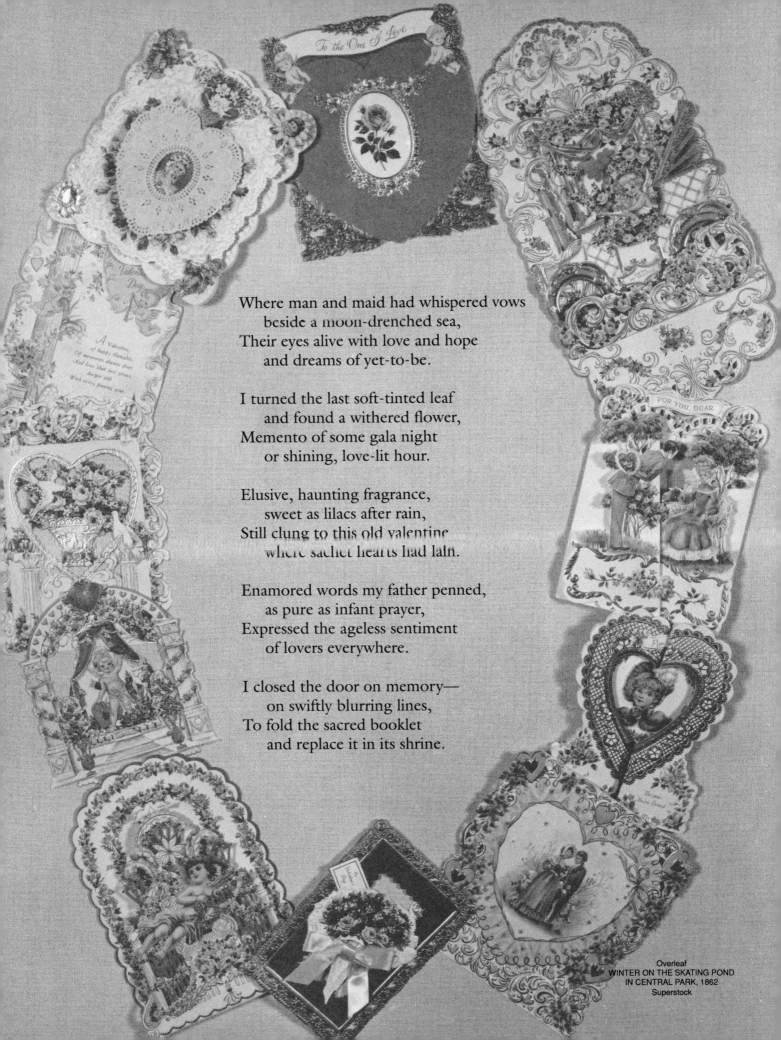

Where man and maid had whispered vows
    beside a moon-drenched sea,
Their eyes alive with love and hope
    and dreams of yet-to-be.

I turned the last soft-tinted leaf
    and found a withered flower,
Memento of some gala night
    or shining, love-lit hour.

Elusive, haunting fragrance,
    sweet as lilacs after rain,
Still clung to this old valentine
    where sachet hearts had lain.

Enamored words my father penned,
    as pure as infant prayer,
Expressed the ageless sentiment
    of lovers everywhere.

I closed the door on memory—
    on swiftly blurring lines,
To fold the sacred booklet
    and replace it in its shrine.

Overleaf
WINTER ON THE SKATING POND
IN CENTRAL PARK, 1862
Superstock

50 YEARS AGO

"Roses Are Red..."

Good morrow! 'Tis Saint Valentine Day
All in the morrow betime,
And I a maid at your window
To be your valentine.

Thus, in *Hamlet*, did Ophelia sing. Shakespeare, as well as Chaucer, Drayton, Cowper, Spenser and many others wrote the praises of Cupid, with his darts and quiver.

Saint Valentine Day is approaching, that day so close to spring in the Northern Hemisphere, with its message of love and hope.

The custom of paying homage to Cupid and one's own true love dates back to the early Roman days, when Valentino, a handsome, dashing youth, suffered martyrdom, being crucified upon the Appian Way. Legend has it, that while awaiting execution, he formed a friendship with the blind daughter of his jailer, and in a message of farewell written to her on the eve of his death, signed it "From your Valentine."

And from this message the custom of valentine cards and greetings has grown, with each age refining the valentine to suit its tastes and needs. The valentines of history are as varied as the people and times that produced them.

In old England we find fine examples of lace paper work and embossing with beautifully applied motifs of rare delicacy. Earlier valentines, appearing about 1780, were drawn and colored by hand, then produced in monochrome and later in lithograph.

To the English stationers of the early nineteenth century we owe a debt of gratitude, for one vied with the other in producing beautiful paper lace work. The makers' names are stamped on the valentine, sometimes more than once, to show their pride in their fine achievement. The marks are small, hidden, and afford collectors much fun.

The "Mirror" valentine was extremely popular, when the lady fair lifted up the "Look at my

The rose will cease to blow,
The eagle turn a dove,
The stream will cease to flow,
'Ere I will cease to love.

beloved" in the center of the missive and found her image in the tiny mirror. One very lovely one was done by the ornamental stationer to King George IV in 1824. The tiny verse in copperplate reads:

The rose will cease to blow,
The eagle turn a dove,
The stream will cease to flow,
Ere I will cease to love.

The "Wafer" valentine, with the wafer center made of flour and gelatin, comes in many forms, and it is to be wondered that such a tiny piece of brittleness has withstood so many years. The most beautiful of the wafer variety was done with an exquisite lace border, the white wafer upon a lace square, delicately decorated with a spray of flowers.

The floral valentines are a delight, with their many varieties. Delicate leaves and flowers of velvet applied in charming circlets and bouquets and all the old flowers of England are as fresh today as when they were done over 100 years ago.

For the damsel or swain who could not afford these greetings, beautiful lace-banded paper and lace-edged envelopes were made and greetings were written in tiny letters. Sweet indeed are some of these treasured old greetings.

Yet just as sweet are our own valentines. The day is still much feted, with valentine flowers, sweets, and telegrams. Western Union sent out 600,000 valentine messages last year. And though today's valentines may not seem as elaborate as those of days past, the messages, and the love behind them, are the same.

So let us always observe this quaint old custom with its messages of sentiment, and let us treasure our own modern valentines as we do those of years and centuries gone by.

From *The Christian Science Monitor Magazine*, February 1941.
Old-fashioned valentine photos courtesy of UPI/Bettmann.

WINTER EVENING

Anna M. Priestly

The white wolf of winter nips my heels;
The snarling wind, with bared fangs,
    stands at bay
Or stealthily pursues its trackless way;
The inmost fiber of my being feels
Its icy breath. Across the landscape steals
Twilight's approaching shadow, cold
    and gray.
Wild spectral shapes before my vision sway
As trees join recklessly in dizzy reels.

Invitingly, a door is swung aside;
A friendly circle breaks to let me in
To swift forgetfulness of night and storm.
In this room, spacious as a friend's
    heart is wide,
Lit by the smiles of those who are akin,
The whole world, suddenly, seems bright
    and warm.

Tell Me of Your Love

Clarence B. Campbell

I could not do so in a thousand years,
A thousand years of happiness and tears.
And if each year could boast a thousand days,
And each day show a thousand different ways
To speak my thoughts in every language known,
Elaborating on this theme alone,
I could not make you understand what lies
Beyond all understanding, what defies
Translation into any form of art.
I cannot brush the motions of my heart
On canvas, play them on the stage, display
Them in a case of words. I only pray
That sometime, at the edge of dreams, you may
Draw close to what I wish so much to say.

Winter Trees

Mary E. Linton

If I had never seen the leaves return
To branches just as cold and dead as these,
This waiting heart would find it hard to learn
That life still throbs in winter's barren trees.

But I have watched new April touch the bough
That cold November wind left desolate,
And memory brings reassurance now;
There is a time when growing things must wait.

Perhaps that is the thing that helps them grow,
Makes them reach deeper for an inner strength,
Tests every fiber so that life may flow
Through sturdy channels when spring
    comes at length.

Out of the faith that lives in winter trees
Hope builds bright banners for a
    springtime breeze.

BITS & PIECES

I crown thee king of intimate delights;
Fireside enjoyments, home-born happiness,
And all the comforts that the lowly roof
Of undisturbed retirement, and the hours
Of long uninterrupted evening know.

Cowper

If winter comes, can spring be far behind?

Percy Bysshe Shelley

All flowers of spring are not May's own;
The crocus cannot often kiss her;
The snow-drop, ere she comes, has flown;
The earliest violets always miss her.

Lucy Larcom

70

Blessings may appear under the shape of pains, losses, and disappointments, but let him have patience, and he will see them in their proper figure.

Addison

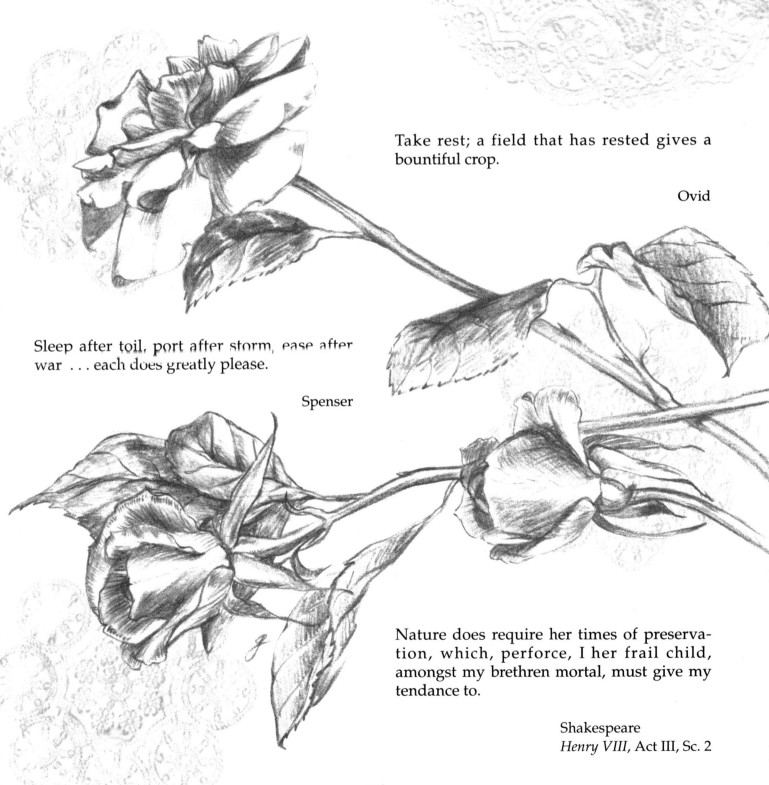

Take rest; a field that has rested gives a bountiful crop.

Ovid

Sleep after toil, port after storm, ease after war . . . each does greatly please.

Spenser

Nature does require her times of preservation, which, perforce, I her frail child, amongst my brethren mortal, must give my tendance to.

Shakespeare
Henry VIII, Act III, Sc. 2

A Winter Scene

Harriet Leila Rourke

Clouds are bleak and gray at dawn
As chill of winter fills the air.
Lovely scenes of autumn fade
To wonder lands of beauty rare.

Snowflakes softly drift to earth
And spread a mantle gleaming white;
They drape the shrubs with tatted lace
And build snow castles overnight.

Windowpanes are etched with frost
Like chapel spires rising high
And birds seek shelter from the cold
Their feathers ruffled and awry.

But winter must not tarry long,
Springtime zephyrs gently blow
Robin redbreast chirps "Farewell,"
And flowers steal up through the snow.

FROM MY
G·A·R·D·E·N
JOURNAL

Deana Duck

Everyone deserves a pot of bright red tulips blooming in the kitchen come Valentine's Day. And—to lend a touch of spring to cold winter mornings—cheerful masses of white and yellow narcissus in every room.

While we're at it, let's toss in some delicate pink and lavender hyacinths to get us through March.

This out-of-season blooming celebration is part of what I call my "Winter Survival Kit." When I lived in long-winter, Zone 3 climates, it always got me through the bleakest, most blustery days and helped me hang on till the robins arrived.

But I have always had a problem with the phrase "forcing bulbs." It sounds so authoritarian—so demanding! I prefer to think of it as "liberating blossoms." After all, without a little assistance, the poor things would have to wait out the entire winter inside a cold, dark bulb.

Persuading bulbs to burst into bloom in advance of schedule takes some planning; if you want blooms in January, you have to get to work in October!

It helps to know something about the life cycle of bulb plants. All true bulbs flower and then spend the next several weeks absorbing energy from the sun through their foliage. As the foliage withers in warm weather, nutrients are transferred to the bulb to replenish its food stocks and ready it for producing a new flower the following season. Once the bulb has been fed, the plant goes dormant.

A new flower cannot be produced until the bulb breaks dormancy. In most bulbs, dormancy can only be broken if the plant spends a specific period of time in the 35 to 45 degree temperature range.

So, to set free the little blossom embryos sleeping inside each bulb, we simply have to chill the dormant bulbs for several weeks, then plant and wait for the magic to happen. If a few bulbs are started in batches about two weeks apart, you can have something in bloom from January until after Easter.

The whole chilling process takes about fourteen weeks. Bulbs chilled longer than this will produce long stems that may have difficulty supporting the weight of the bulb. Bulbs cooled for less time will have short, stubby stems.

For the first few weeks, bulbs can be stored loosely in perforated paper bags in a refrigerator. After this, they have to be planted in pots so that roots can form. If you do not have room in the refrigerator for the pots, use an unheated garage or back porch. Bulbs can also be chilled on an apartment balcony or patio. Pack them in vermiculite in a picnic cooler to protect them from the wind. After planting, remove the vermiculite and set the containers in the cooler or in cardboard boxes insulated with newspapers. They will stay cool, but they will not freeze.

If the temperature drops below 20°, simply place a five-inch stack of newspapers under the cooler, or a heavy blanket over the top, and let the bulbs continue to cool. Unless the temperature drops to several degrees below zero and stays there, the cooler will be adequate protection.

Tulips, lilies, and other bulbs do best when planted in pots of loose, well-draining soil mixed with equal parts of peat and sand, or generous amounts of vermiculite or perlite. Narcissus, crocuses, and hyacinths do well when planted in water-filled containers, but can also be planted in pots of soil. A six-inch pot will hold, on average, about three hyacinths, six tulips or daffodils, and a dozen or more crocuses.

Place the tops of the bulbs even with the rim of the pot when planting, then fill in space around the bulbs with more loosely packed soil. Water two or three times to let the soil settle, but do not pack it down tightly or the roots will have difficulty growing.

Once the bulbs are in pots, they can be left alone until the fourteen weeks have passed and it is time for blooming.

Regardless of the planting method you select for your bulbs, make sure to chill them in the container until forcing time. By then the roots will have formed and the bulbs will have begun to sprout. At that point, you can set the pots in a warm sunny spot and the bulbs will bloom within three to four weeks.

Even though icicles may be hanging from your eaves, your home will be transformed into a fragrant spring garden!

Deana Deck lives in Nashville, Tennessee, where her garden column is a regular feature in the Tennessean.

As the Heart
Remembers Spring

Betty W. Stoffel

Some will be remembered
For the fortunes of their fame,
And some will be remembered
For the naming of a name,
But you will be remembered
As the heart remembers spring,
As the mind remembers beauty,
And the soul each lovely thing.

You have been skies of April,
And fragrant breath of May,
And like the season's coming,
Warm-spirited and gay.
You have given freely
Of the beauty of your heart,
And you have made of friendship
Not a gesture but an art.

You have been as selfless
In the gracious things you do
As the sun that shares its kisses,
As the night that shares its dew.
You have planted roses
In lives that lay so bare,
You have sown encouragement
To those who knew despair.

By your spirit's inner beauty
In every lovely thing,
You will be remembered
As the heart remembers spring!

Photo Opposite
SNOWDROP AND ACONITE
Gottlieb Hampfler Studios

ONLY LOVE

Ann Thompson Jester

Only love will last.
An old homeplace
Disintegrates when years
Have robbed it of its laughter,
Joy, and tears;
Yet from its memoried ruins
Love will rise
To live and shine again
In someone's eyes.

The year at spring
Is beautiful and young.
Before it's gone
A million songs are sung
By silver-throated birds.
Inconsequential is the
Lack of words,

For their melodies
The poet sings,
And love, the source,
From whence all beauty springs
Survives in time
Through words and song.
It matters not if seasons,
Short or long,
Fade into destiny.
In time against all odds
Love still remains—
Perfect and pure
As God ordained it to be.

Only love will last
Long after summer rains
Subside and winter winds are still.
Though mountains soon grow bare
And river beds run dry, there will
Out of love's arid desert bloom
A lasting flower—love,
With rarest, sweet perfume.

Readers' Forum

Just had to write to let you know how we have utilized your wonderful magazine. We are a small poetry group at an adult day health center for the elderly and handicapped. We formed a group using your magazine. Our topic was country and we read your issue of Volume 46 number 4 with the goal of writing a poem. We hope you will enjoy our "Country Memories" as much as we enjoyed putting them together.

Windsor House Poetry Group
Windsor House Adult Day Health Center
Somerville, Massachusetts

Country Memories

Sitting under a tree
Reading my bible, eating raisins,
Seeing all the animals, and
Looking at the flowers.
Remembering the green fields with
Dandelion blossoms blowing in the breeze.

I remember going on vacation
To my aunt's farm,
Amazed at the apple trees,
Seeing deer, rabbits, and even a bear.
Wild flower seeds just being thrown;
What a beautiful sight when they are grown.

I'm remembering the big rocks
Where I used to sit and see the world
As I then thought,
Watching the old farmer bring down
His cows to my pasture.
The old barn with the wild grass growing high;
These things will remain in our hearts forever:
Country memories.

Members of the Windsor House Poetry Group,
Somerville, Massachusetts

Editor's Note: We have received several inquiries about the painting featured on the cover of our 1990 Christmas *Ideals*. The artist is Linda Nelson Stocks, and her work is available through Linda Nelson Stocks Studios in Fisher, Illinois.

YESTERDAY IN AMERICA
Remember the "good old days"? The editors of IDEALS are planning a book about American life in the 1920s, '30s, and '40s and we need readers to share their experiences. We invite you to submit short essays of 500 words or less about your own experiences during this era for possible publication. Please send material to: Yesterday in America, Ideals Publishing Corporation, P. O. Box 148000, Nashville, TN 37214-8000. Send copies only; manuscripts cannot be returned.

Statement of ownership, management, and circulation (Required by 39 U. S. C. 3685), of IDEALS, published eight times a year in February, March, May, June, August, September, November, and December at Nashville, Tennessee, for September 1990. Publisher, Patricia A. Pingry; Editor, Nancy Skarmeas; Managing Editor, as above; Owner, Egmont U. S., Inc., wholly owned subsidiary of The Egmont H. Petersen Foundation, VOGNMAGERGADE 11, 1148 Copenhagen, K, Denmark. The known bondholders, mortgage, and other securities holders owning or holding 1 percent or more of total amount of bonds, mortgages, and other securities are: None. Average no. copies each issue during preceding 12 months: Total no. copies printed (Net Press Run) 232,512. Paid circulation 43,717. Mail subscription 168,290. Total paid circulation 212,007. Free distribution 983. Total distribution 212,990. Actual no. copies of single issue published nearest to filing date: Total no. copies printed (Net Press Run) 186, 452. Paid circulation 13,272. Mail subscription 164,999. Total paid circulation 178,271. Free distribution 336. Total distribution 178,607. I certify that the statements made by me above are correct and complete. Rose A. Yates, Vice President, Direct Marketing Systems and Operations.